Henry Drummond

What is a Christian?

The Study of the Bible

Henry Drummond

What is a Christian?
The Study of the Bible

ISBN/EAN: 9783337171506

Printed in Europe, USA, Canada, Australia, Japan

Cover: Foto ©ninafisch / pixelio.de

More available books at **www.hansebooks.com**

HAT IS A CHRISTIAN?

What is a Christian? The Study of The Bible; A Talk on Books

By
Henry Drummond

Philadelphia
Henry Altemus

WHAT IS A CHRISTIAN?

YOUNG men are learning to respect more, perhaps, than ever young men have done, the word "Christian." I have seen the time when it was synonymous with cant and unreality and strained feeling and sanctimoniousness. But although that day is not quite passed yet, it is passing. I heard this definition the other day of a Christian man by a cynic — "A Christian man is a man whose great aim in life is a selfish desire to save his own soul, who, in order to do that, goes regularly to church, and whose supreme hope is to get to Heaven when he dies." This reminds one of Professor Huxley's examination paper in which the question was put—"What is a lobster?" One student replied that a lobster was a red fish, which moves backwards. The examiner noted that this was a very good answer, but for three things. In the first place a lobster was not a fish; second it was not red; and third it did not move backwards. If there is anything that a Christian is not, it is one who has a selfish desire to save his own soul. The one thing which Christianity tries to extirpate from a man's nature is selfishness, even though it be the losing of his own soul.

Christianity, as we understand it from Christ, appeals to the generous side of a young man's nature, and not to the selfish side. In the new version of the New Testament the word "soul" is always translated in this connection by the word "life." That marks a revolution in the popular theology, and it will make a revolution in every Young Man's Christian Association in the country where it comes to be seen that a man's Christianity does not consist in merely saving his own soul, but in sanctifying and purifying the lives of his fellow-men. We are told in the New Testament that Christianity is leaven, and "leaven" comes from the same root-word as lever, meaning that which raises up, which elevates; and a Christian young man is a man who raises up or elevates the lives of those round about him. We are also told that Christianity is salt, and salt is that which saves from corruption. What is it that saves the life of the world from being utterly rotten, but the Christian elements that are in it? Matthew Arnold has said, "Show me ten square miles in any part of the world outside Christianity where the life of man and the purity of woman are safe, and I will give Christianity up." In no part of the world is there any such ten square miles outside Christianity. Christian men are the salt of the earth in the most literal sense. They, and they alone, keep the world from utter destruction.

I want to say a word here about the Young Men's Christian Associations. Many have criticised them. They have been the target for a great deal of abuse. Many of the best young men have sneered at them, and turned up their noses at them, and denounced them. I am speaking with absolute sympathy and respect, and even enthusiasm, for Young Men's Christian Associations. But I will turn for one instant upon those men who turn against them, and tell them that it is not breadth that leads them to do that, but what one might call the narrowness of breadth — that breadth which denounces intolerance, and which is itself too intolerant to tolerate intolerance. And, as some one says, it is easier to criticise the best thing superbly than to do the smallest thing indifferently.

It is very easy to criticise the methods and aims and men of the Young Men's Christian Associations. If, instead of looking on and criticising those who know a thing or two, those who think they are wiser, and that they have the whole truth, would throw themselves in among others and back them and try to work alongside of them, they would get perhaps their breadth tempered by earnestness and by zeal, because the narrow man has much to contribute to the Christian cause, perhaps more than the broad man. But it needs all kinds of people to make a world; it needs all kinds of people to make a church, and every type of young men a Christian Association; and the greatest mistake of all is to have every man stamped in the same stamp, so that if you met him in a railway train one hundred miles off, you would know him as a Y. M. C. A. man. I would like to find many who would not wear the badge so pronouncedly, that every one should know them at a glance.

There is only one great character in the world that can really draw out all that is best in man. He is so far above all others in influencing men for good that He stands alone. That man was the founder of Christianity. To be a Christian man is to have that character for our ideal in life, to live under its influence, to do what He would wish us to do, to live the kind of life He would have lived in our house, and had He our day's routine to go through. It would not, perhaps, alter the forms of our life, but it would alter the spirit and aims and motives of our life, and the Christian man is he who in that sense lives under the influence of Jesus Christ.

Now, there is nothing that a young man wants for his ideal that is not found in Christ. You would be surprised when you come to know who

Christ is, if you have not thought much about it, to find how He will fit in with all human needs, and call out all that is best in man.   The highest and manliest character that ever lived was Christ.   One incident I often think of and wonder.   You remember, when He hung upon the cross, there was handed up to Him a vessel containing a stupefying drug, supplied by a kind society of ladies in Jerusalem, who always sent it to criminals when being executed.   And that stupefying drug was handed up to Christ's lips.   And we read, "When he tasted thereof He would not drink."   I have always thought that one of the most heroic actions I have ever read of   But that.

was only one very small side of Christ's nature. He can be everything that a man wants. Paul tells us that if we live in Christ we are changed into His image. All that a man has to do, then, to be like Christ, is simply to live in friendship with Christ, and the character follows.

But it is only one of the aims of Christianity to make the best men. The next thing Christ wants to do is to make the best world. And He tries to make the best world by setting the best men loose upon the world to influence it and reflect Him upon it. In 1874 a religious movement began in Edinburgh University among the students themselves, that has since

spread to some of the best academic
institutions in America.   The students
have a hall, and there they meet on
Sundays, or occasionally on week-days,
to hear addresses from their profes-
sors, or from outside eminent men, on
Christian topics.   There is no com-
mittee; there are no rules; there are
no reports.   Every meeting is held
strictly in private, and any attempt to
pose before the world is sternly dis-
couraged.   No paragraphs are put into
the journals; no addresses are reported.
The meetings are private, quiet, ear-
nest, and whatsoever student likes may
attend them.   That is all.   It is not
an organization in the ordinary sense,
it is a "leaven."   In all the schools

it is the best men who take most
part in the movement, and among the
schools it is the medical side which
furnishes the greatest number of students to the meetings. Some of the
most zealous have taken high honors
in their examinations, and some have
been in the first class of university
athletes. It is not a movement that
has laid hold of weak or worthless
students whom nobody respects, but
one that is maintained by the best men
in every department. The first benefit
is to the students themselves. Take
Edinburgh, with about 4000 students
drawn from all parts of the world, and
living in rooms with no one caring for
them. Taken away from the moral

support of their previous surroundings, they went to the bad in hundreds. It is now found that through this movement they work better, and that a greater percentage pass honorably through the university portals into life. The religious meetings, it is to be observed, are never allowed to interfere with the work of the students. The second result is to be seen in what are called university settlements. A few men will band themselves together and rent a house in the lower parts of the city and live there. They do no preaching, no formal evangelization work; but they help the sick and they arrange smoking concerts, and contribute to the amusement of their neighbors. They

simply live with the people, and trust
that their example will produce a good
effect. Three years ago they printed
and distributed among themselves the
following "Programme of Christianity:" — "To bind up the broken-
hearted, to give liberty to the captives,
to comfort all that mourn, to give
beauty for ashes, the garment of praise
for the spirit of heaviness." I suppose
there are few of us with broken hearts,
but there are other people in the world
besides ourselves, and underneath all
the gayety of the city there is not a
street in which there are not men and
women with broken hearts. Who is
to help these people? No one can lift
them up in any way except those who

are living the life of Christ, and it is their privilege and business to bind up the broken-hearted.

I want to urge the claims of the Christian ministry on the strength and talent of our youth. I find a singular want of men in the Christian ministry, and I think it would be at least worth while for some of you to look around, to look at the men who are not filling the churches, to look at the needs of the crowds who throng the streets, and see if you could do better with your life than throw yourself into that work. The advantage of the ministry is that a man's whole life can be thrown into the carrying out of that programme without any deduction. Another advantage of the ministry is that it is so poorly paid that a man is not tempted to cut a dash and shine in the world, but can be meek and lowly in heart, like his Master. It is enough for a servant to be like his master, and there is a great attraction in seeking obscurity, even isolation, if one can be following the highest ideal.

With regard to the question, how you shall begin the Christian life, let me remind you that theology is the most abstruse thing in the world, but that practical religion is the simplest thing. If any of you want to know how to begin to be a Christian, all I can say is that you should begin to do the next thing you find to be done as

Christ would have done it.   If you
follow Christ the "old man" will die
of atrophy, and the "new man" will
grow day by day under His abiding
friendship.

THE STUDY OF THE BIBLE.

THE STUDY OF THE BIBLE.

I WILL give a note or two, pretty much by way of refreshing the memory about the Bible and how to look at it.

First: *The Bible came out of religion, not religion out of the Bible.* The Bible is a product of religion, not a cause of it. The war literature of America, which culminated, I suppose, in the publication of President Grant's life, came out of the war; the war did not

come out of the literature.   And so in
the distant past, there flowed among
the nations of heathendom a small
warm stream, like the Gulf Stream in
the cold Atlantic — a small stream of
religion; and now and then at intervals, men, carried along by this stream,
uttered themselves in words.   The his-
torical books came out of facts; the
devotional books came out of experiences; the letters came out of circumstances; and the Gospels came out of
all three.   That is where the Bible
came from.   It came out of religion;
religion did not come out of the Bible.
You see the difference.   The religion
is not, then, in the writing alone; but
in those facts, experiences, circum-

stances, in the history and development of a people led and taught by God. And it is not the words that are inspired so much as the men.

Secondly : *These men were authors; they were not pens.* Their individuality comes out on every page they wrote. They were different in mental and literary style; in insight; and even the same writer differs at different times. II. Thessalonians, for example, is considerably beneath the level of Romans, and III. John is beneath the level of I. John. A man is not always at his best. These writers did not know they were writing a Bible.

Third : *The Bible is not a book; it is a library.* It consists of sixty-six books.   It is a great convenience, but in some respects a great misfortune, that these books have always been bound up together and given out as one book to the world, when they are not; because that has led to endless mistakes in theology and in practical life.

Fourth : These books, which make up this library, written at intervals of hundreds of years, were collected after the last of the writers was dead — long after — by human hands.   Where were the books ?   Take the New Testament. There were four lives of Christ.   One was in Rome; one was in Southern Italy; one was in Palestine; one in Asia Minor.   There were twenty-one

letters. Five were in Greece and
Macedonia ; five in Asia ; one in
Rome. The rest were in the pockets
of private individuals. Theophilus had
acts. They were collected undesignedly. For example, the letter to the
Galatians was written to the Church
in Galatia. Somebody would make a
copy or two, and put it into the hands
of the members of the different
churches, and they would find their
way not only to the churches in Galatia, but after an interval to nearly
all the churches. In those days the
Christians scattered up and down
through the world, exchanged copies
of those letters, very much as geolo-
gists up and down the world exchange

specimens of minerals at the present time, or entomologists exchange specimens of butterflies. And after a long time a number of the books began to be pretty well known. In the third century the New Testament consisted of the following books: the four Gospels, Acts, thirteen letters of Paul, I. John, I. Peter; and in addition, the Epistles of Barnabas and Hermas. This was not called the New Testament, but the Christian Library. Then these last books were discarded. They ceased to be regarded as upon the same level as the others. In the fourth century the canon was closed — that is to say, a list was made up of the books which were to be regarded as canonical. And then long after that they were stitched together and made up into one book — hundreds of years after that. Who made up the complete list? It was never formally made up. The bishops of the different churches would draw up a list each of the books that they thought ought to be put into this Testament. The churches also would give their opinion. Sometimes councils would meet and talk it over — discuss it. Scholars like Jerome would investigate the authenticity of the different documents, and there came to be a general consensus of the churches on the matter. But no formal closing of the canon was ever attempted.

And lastly : All religions have their sacred books, just as the Christians have theirs. Why is it necessary to remind ourselves of that ? If you ask a man why he believes such and such a thing, he will tell you, Because it is in the Bible. If you ask him, " How do you know the Bible is true?" he will probably reply, " Because it says so." Now, let that man remember that the sacred books of all the other religions make the same claim; and while it is quite enough among ourselves to talk about a thing being true because it is in the Bible, we come in contact with outsiders, and we have to meet the skepticism of the day. We must go far deeper than that. The religious books of the other religions claim to be far more divine in their origin than do ours. For example, the Mohammedans claim for the Koran — a large section of them, at least — that it was uncreated, and that it lay before the throne of God from the beginning of time. They claim it was put in the hands of the angel Gabriel, who brought it down to Mahomet, and dictated it to him, and allowed him at long intervals to have a look at the original book itself — bound with silk and studded with precious stones. That is a claim of much higher Divinity than we claim for our book ; and if we simply have to rely upon the Bible's testimony to its own verity, it is for the same reason the Mohammedan would have you believe his book, and the Hindu would have you put your trust in the Vedas. That is why thorough Bible study is of such importance. We can get to the bottom of truth in itself, and be able to give a reason for the faith that is in us.

Now may I give you, before I stop, just a couple of examples of how the Bible came out of religion, and not religion out of the Bible? Take one of the letters. Just see how it came out of the circumstances of the time. The first of the letters that was written will do very well as an example. It is the 1st Epistle to the Thessalonians. In the year 52 Paul went to Europe.

He spent three Sundays in Thessalonica, created a great disturbance by his preaching, and a riot sprang up, and his life was in danger. He was smuggled out of the city at night — not, however, before having founded a small church. He was unable to go back to Thessalonica, although he tried it two or three times ; but he wrote a letter. That is the first letter to the Thessalonians. You see how it sprang out of the circumstances of the time. Take a second example. Let us take one of the lives of Christ. Suppose you take the life recorded by Mark. Now, from internal evidences you can make out quite clearly how it was written, by whom it was written, and to whom it was written. You understand at once it was written to a Roman public. If I were writing a letter to a red Indian I would make it very different from a letter I would write to a European. Now, Mark puts in a number of points which he would not if he had been writing to Greeks. For example, Mark almost never quotes prophecy. The Romans did not know anything about prophecy. Then, he gives little explanation of Jewish customs. When I was writing home I had to give some little explanations of American customs — for example, Commencement Day. When Mark writes to Rome about things happening farther East, he gives elaborate explanations.   Again, Mark is fond of Latin words — writing to the Latins, who could understand them. He talks about " centurion," " prætorium," and others.   Then, he always turns Jewish money into Roman money, just as I should say a book, if I were writing to Europe about it, cost two shillings, instead of fifty cents.   Mark, for example, says, "two mites, which make a codrantes."   He refers to the coins which the Romans knew.   In these ways we find out that the Bible came out of the circumstances and the places and the times in which it was written.   Then if we will we can learn where Mark got his information, to a large extent.   It is an extremely interesting study. I should like to refer to Gocet's "New Testament Studies," where you will get this worked out. Let me just indicate to you how these sources of information are arrived at — the principal sources of information. There are a number of graphic touches in the book which indicate an eye-witness. Mark himself could not have been the eye-witness; and yet there are a number of graphic touches which show that he got his account from an eye-witness. You will find them, for example, in Mark iv. 38; x. 50; vi. 31; vii. 34. You will find also graphic touches indicating an ear-witness — as if the voice lingered in the mind of the writer. For example, the retention of Aramaic in v. 41 ; and in vii. 34 — "*Talitha cumi ;* Damsel, I say unto thee, arise." He retained the Aramaic words Christ said, as I would say in Scotland, "My wee lassie, rise up." The very words lingered in his ear, and he put them in the original. Then there are occasional phrases indicating the moral impression produced — v. 15 ; x. 24; x. 32. Now, Mark himself was not either the eye-witness or ear-witness. There is internal evidence that he got his information from Peter. We know very well that Mark was an intimate friend of Peter's. When Peter came to Mark's house in Jerusalem, after he got out of prison, the very servant knew his voice, so that he must have been well known in the house. Therefore he was a friend of Mark's. The coloring and notes seem to be derived from Peter. There is a sense of wonder and admiration which you find all through the book, very like Peter's way of looking at things — i. 27; i. 33; i. 45; ii. 12; v. 42; and a great many others. But, still more interesting, Mark quotes the words, "Get thee behind. Me, Satan," which were said to Peter's shame, but he omits the preceding words said to his honor — "Thou art Peter. On this rock," and so on. Peter had learned to be humble when he was telling Mark about it. Compare Mark viii.

27–33, with Matthew's account — xvi. 13–33. Mark also omits the fine achievement of Peter — walking on the lake. When Peter was talking to Mark, he never said anything about it. Compare vi. 50 with Matthew's account — xiv. 28. And Mark alone records the two warnings given to Peter by the two cock-crowings, making his fall the more inexcusable. See Mark xiv. 30; also the 68th verse and the 72d. Peter did not write the book; we know that, because Peter's style is entirely different. None of the four Gospels have the names of the writers attached to them. We have had to find all these things out; but Mark's Gospel is obviously made up of notes from Peter's evangelistic addresses.

So we see from these simple examples how human a book the Bible is, and how the Divinity in it has worked through human means. The Bible, in fact, has come out of religion; not religion out of the Bible.

A TALK ON BOOKS.

No book is worth anything which is not worth much nor is it serviceable until it has been read, and re-read, and loved, and loved again; and marked so that you can refer to the passages you want in it, as a soldier can seize the weapons he needs in any armory, or a housewife bring the piece she needs from her store.

— JOHN RUSKIN.

Except a living man, there is nothing more wonderful than a book! — A message to us from the dead — from human souls whom we never saw, who lived, perhaps, thousands of miles away, and yet these, or those little sheets of paper, speak to us, amuse us, comfort us, open their hearts to us as brothers.

— CHAS. KINGSLEY.

Good books, like good friends, are few and chosen; the more select the more enjoyable.

— A. BRONSON ALCOTT.

46

A TALK ON BOOKS.

M Y object at this time is to give encouragement and help to the " duffers," the class of " hopeful duffers." Brilliant students have every help, but second-class students are sometimes neglected and disheartened. I have great sympathy " with the duffers," because I was only a second-rate student myself. The subject of my talk with you is

BOOKS.

A gentleman in Scotland who has an excellent library has placed on one side of the room his heavy sombre tomes, and over those shelves the form of an owl. On the other side of the room are arranged the lighter books, and over these is the figure of a bird known in Scotland as "the dipper." This is a most sensible division. The "owl books" are to be mastered,—the great books, such as Gibbon's "Rome," Butler's "Analogy," Dorner's "Person of Christ," and text-books of philosophy and science. Every student should master one or two, at least, of such "owl books," to exercise his faculties, and give him concentrativeness. I do not intend to linger at this side of the library, but will cross over to the "dipper books," which are for occasional reading—for stimulus, for guidance, recreation. I will be

AUTOBIOGRAPHICAL.

When I was a student in lodgings I began to form a library, which I arranged along the mantelshelf of my room. It did not contain many books; but it held as many as some students could afford to purchase, and if wisely chosen, as many as one could well use. My first purchase was a volume of extracts from Ruskin's works, which then in their complete form were very costly. Ruskin taught me to use my eyes. Men are born blind as bats or kittens, and it is long before men's eyes are opened; some men never learn to see as long as they live. I often wondered, if there was a Creator, why He had not made the world more beautiful. Would not crimson and scarlet colors have been far richer than green and browns? But Ruskin taught me to see the world as it is, and it soon became a new world to me, full of charm and loveliness. Now I can linger beside a ploughed field and revel in the affluence of color and shade which are to be seen in the newly turned furrows, and I gaze in wonder at the liquid amber of the two feet of air above the brown earth. Now the colors and shades of the woods are a delight, and at every turn my eyes are surprised at fresh charms. The rock which I had supposed to be naked I saw clothed with lichens — patches of color — marvellous organisms, frail as the ash of a cigar, thin as brown paper, yet growing and fructifying in spite of wind and rain, of scorching sun and biting frost. I owe much to Ruskin for teaching me to see.

Next on my mantelshelf was Emerson. I discovered Emerson for myself. When I asked what Emerson was, one authority pronounced him a great man; another as confidently wrote him down a humbug. So I silently stuck to Emerson. Carlyle I could not read. After wading through a page of Carlyle I felt as if I had been whipped. Carlyle scolded too much for my taste and he seemed to me a great man gone delirious. But in Emerson I found what I would fain have sought in Carlyle; and, moreover, I was soothed and helped. Emerson taught me to see with the mind.

Next on my shelf came two or three volumes of George Eliot's works, from which I gained some knowledge and a furthur insight into many philosophical and social questions. But my chief debt to George Eliot at that time was that she introduced me to pleasant characters—nice people—and especially to one imaginary young lady whom I was in love with one whole winter, and it diverted my mind in solitude. A good novel is a valuable acquisition, and it supplies companionship of a pleasant kind.

Amongst my small residue of books I must name Channing's works. Before I read Channing I doubted whether there was a God; at least I would rather have believed that there were no God. After becoming acquainted with Channing I could believe there was a God, and I was glad to believe in Him, for I felt drawn to the good and gracious Sovereign of all things. Still, I needed further what I found in F. W. Robertson, the British officer in the pulpit — bravest, truest of men — who dared to speak what he believed at all hazards. From Robertson I learned that God is human; that we may have fellowship with Him, because He sympathizes with us.

One day as I was looking over my mantelshelf library, it suddenly struck me that all these authors of mine were heretics — these were dangerous books. Undesignedly I had found stimulus and help from teachers who were not credited by orthodoxy. And I have since found that much of the good to be got from books is to be gained from authors often classed as dangerous, for these provoke inquiry, and exercise one's powers. Towards the end of my shelf I had one or two humorous works; chief amongst them all being Mark Twain. His humor is peculiar; broad exaggeration, a sly simplicity, comical situations, and surprising turns of expressions ; but to me it has been a genuine fund of humor. The humorous side of a student's nature needs to be considered, and where it is undeveloped, it should

be cultivated. I have known many in-
stances of good students who seemed to
have no sense of humor.

I will not recommend any of my fav-
orite books to another; they have done
me good, but they might not suit another
man. Every man must discover his own
books; but when he has found what fits
in with his tastes, what stimulates him
to thought, what supplies a want in his
nature, and exalts him in conception and
feelings, that is the book for the student,
be what it may. This brings me to
speak of

THE FRIENDSHIP OF BOOKS.

To fall in love with a good book is
one of the greatest events that can

befall us.   It is to have a new influence
pouring itself into our life, a new teach-
er to inspire and refine us, a new friend
to be by our side always, who, when life
grows narrow and weary, will take us
into his wider and calmer and higher
world.   Whether it be biography intro-
ducing us to some humble life made
great by duty done ; or history, opening
vistas into the movements and destinies
of nations that have passed away; or
poetry making music of all the common
things around us, and filling the fields,
and the skies, and the work of the city
and the cottage with eternal meanings
—whether it be these, or story books, or
religious books, or science, no one can
become the friend even of one good

book without being made wiser and better. Do not think I am going to recommend any such book to you. The beauty of a friend is that we discover him. And we must each taste the books that are accessible to us for ourselves. Do not be disheartened at first if you like none of them. That is possibly their fault, not yours. But search and search till you find what you like. In amazingly cheap form—for a few pence indeed—almost all the best books are now to be had; and I think everyone owes it as a sacred duty to his *mind* to start a little library of his own. How much do we not do for our bodies? How much thought and money do they not cost us? And shall we not think a little, and pay a little, for the clothing and adorning of the imperishable mind? This private library may begin, perhaps, with a single volume, and grow at the rate of one or two a year; but these well-chosen and well-mastered, will become such a fountain of strength and wisdom that each shall be eager to add to his store. A dozen books accumulated in this way may be better than a whole library. Do not be distressed if you do not like time-honored books, or classical works, or recommended books. Choose for yourself; trust yourself; plant yourself on your own instincts; that which is natural for us, that which nourishes us, and gives us appetite, is that which is right for us. We have all different minds, and we are all at different stages of growth. Some other day we may find food in the recommended book, though we should possibly starve on it to-day. The mind develops and changes, and the favorites of this year, also, may one day cease to interest us. Nothing better indeed can happen to us than to lose interest in a book we have often read; for it means that it has done its work upon us, and brought us up to its level, and taught us all it had to teach.

www.ingramcontent.com/pod-product-compliance
Lightning Source LLC
Chambersburg PA
CBHW030858260626
47169CB00008B/2588